The debris in my m

The debris
in my mind

Keith Terry

Keith Terry

ISBN: 10:1517194091
ISBN-13: 978-1517194093

DEDICATION

With thanks to so many people; it is impossible to name them all. However, I must thank family and particularly my wife Louise, without whose love and support these poems would not be written, and I would certainly not be the person I am.

Louise has had much to put up with, particularly during thirty seven years of uncertainty and worry, and perhaps even more during the years after my retirement due to injury.

PREFACE

This collection of my poems
Is the first to be printed.
Perchance they hint at how my life
And attitudes have shifted.

Some poems tell of journeys
Of love, of laughter, life.
Others allude to suffering
Anguish, pain or strife.

Many are glib, often obtuse;
A few are light and frothy.
Some ask questions of you and I,
A couple may make you angry.

Most are formulaic,
Written down in rhyme
Others are more abstract,
And they don't.

'*My first one*' is at the beginning,
I could not leave it out.
It started off my visceral verse
Of that there is no doubt.

It exorcised my demons
Stopped nightmares, yet shed tears.
Whilst others confirm my happiness
But still address my fears.

The quality certainly varies,
But they're just debris from my mind.
They're the thoughts and often ramblings
Of which I have become resigned.

I digress right now, meander,
I should say, "Enjoy, read on".
These snippets of my inner thoughts
From the beginning and '*My first one*'.

CONTENTS

ACKNOWLEDGMENTS

I should also acknowledge and thank Catherine Roth who was my tutor at Tamworth College. It was because of her efforts and encouragement, I wrote 'My first one'.

The writing of this poem exorcised many demons for me and, following its penning, ended years of nightmares.

I would, aslo like To; thank my nephewAndrew. And and He knows What four.

My first one

Candice was my first one, back in nineteen seventy eight,
Found murdered in a stairwell, in the flats on an estate.

They sent me there, that fateful day, to preserve the primary scene,
Make sure no-one left the block, if returning, where they'd been.

I looked upon her body, the subject of a rape,
Lying there on that cold hard floor, out of place, behind the tape.

Her Afro hair, her dark brown skin, walls so stark and white,
Contrast sharp and so austere, it did not seem quite right.

The picture of her lying there, position almost foetal,
Life extinguished far too soon, in a manner far too brutal.

I saw me on the news that night, my parents oh so proud,
But I bowed my head and cried again, I'm a bloke, that's not allowed.

Funeral delayed, parents distraught, a family ripped apart.
And others, like ripples on a pond, a list too long to start.

In life I never knew her; we had never even met,
In death our encounter was so short, but Candice I can't forget.

Over my time I've seen some shit; bodies, blood and gore,
During thirty years I've seen too much, I pray to see no more.

Of course there were many others, lives taken or defiled,
Yet it's the image of Candice seared in my mind,
For she was my first dead child.

Summer breeze

Love is like a summer breeze
Arrives quietly whilst you are unaware
Envelops your senses, you have no resistance
Cannot be seen, but you know it is there

With a gentle brush goose bumps encouraged
Consumes you like a chill
A sensation so enigmatic
Solicits an unpreventable thrill

Like a leaf you are carried away
No control over one's directional sense
That insignificant cool summer breeze
Becomes something marvellous, wondrous, intense

Give yourselves up to that soft summer breeze
No emotion synonymous you will learn
The only thing like it in life that is better
Is loving and being loved in return

Safety in numbers

This poem was originally conceived in an attempt to try and convey the tension felt on a live firearms operation. However, like many of my poems, it morphed, as I am inclined to ramble, meander and skew my original intentions.

Subtle contours under account-purchased jackets
Constricted confines
Pounding temples
Hyped anticipation of the plans
Inane chatter
Awkward silences, and yet;
You cannot hear birds.

Hours of forced waiting for one repeated word
The smell of cordite,
Tension, fear
Surging adrenalin preceding ultimate confrontation
Movements seemingly suspended in time, and yet;
You cannot hear birds.

Glinting, flashing stainless steel
Punctured holes between the ribs
Cadavers drained of life
Lie silently on brushed steel tables, and yet;
You cannot hear birds.

Twisted metal
Twisted limbs
Broken bodies, young and old
Intense scrutiny to establish why, and yet;
You cannot hear birds.

The fights
The bottles
The beatings
The visits
Waiting patiently with hope in cubicles, and yet;
You cannot hear birds.

However

No guns
No knives
No wasted lives
I can hear birds.

No blood
No stitches
No screaming bitches
I can hear birds.

No hatred
No violence
No vitriolic vengeance
I can hear birds.

If I can hear birds I have shed former life,
If I can hear birds I know I am safe.
If I can hear birds it is tranquil and calm.
The birds that I hear protect me from harm.
The more birds I hear the safer I'll be,
There is safety in numbers and salvation for me.

Anyone for tennis?

A short story in rhyme of;
the annual international Montalivet tennis tournament.

Preceding the tournament!

A friend of mine named Dinah, thought she would help one day,
My name she scribed upon a list, a tournament to play.

Roland-Garros it is not, but tennis was the game,
I knew that after two days' play I'd never be the same.
I'd played before, back at school, but that was more a skive,
Different this, two days of pain and now I'm fifty five.

Dinah suggested training, perhaps the day before.
But weather somehow intervened, as it began to pour.

Wearing second-hand Reeboks, holding eBay purchased bats,
I could not even find my shorts; I'd be playing in my pants.
So now the clock is ticking, it starts in half an hour.
I'm sitting, praying, rain again, perchance a heavy shower?

It didn't rain.

We started off really well, my partner Pierre and I.
We won the first set six to two, then I began to die.

One six, one six, followed quick, and swiftly on, downhill.
My partner Pierre looked at me; if only looks could kill.
Day one finished, just like me, I showered but not in rain.
My feet they hurt already, but, I've to do it all again.

Day two will start at ten o'clock, Sunday rest being shattered.
I'll pray for rain again tonight, yet does it really matter?

Time for bed.

Following a disturbed night of aching feet and cramp,
I woke to face the second day, feeling like a tramp.
The sun was shining brightly, a pleasant cooling breeze,
Perfect weather for tennis not perfect for my knees.

Aching limbs I took to court, like a man condemned.
This second day commenced at pace will this torture never end?
It didn't, it continued; six one, six one, six one.
Losing matches rapidly my energy was gone.

At half past twelve concluded, it finished with a cheer,
Then I trudged home defeated, in great need of a beer.

Prize ceremony, two o'clock, contestants all applauded,
They cheered and whooped as prizes given, winners were rewarded.
So I was last, that's no surprise, what was that prize of mine?
The satisfaction, taking part, oh, and of course, the wine.

Dinah you've much to answer for, the way you made me run,
But really I wish to thank you, for it was so much fun.

Entry in the tournament next year?
No I don't think so!

Chartres Cathedral

Have you ever visited Chartres? You should, I'll tell you why
It has a bucket list cathedral, a 'must see' before you die
The exterior may be stunning, spire and vista seen from miles
But it's the inside that's so memorable, the vaults, transepts, aisles

It is famous for its labyrinth, set in ancient flagstone floor
More of an extant pathway, one with meaning and much more
This symbolic maze turns and twists, it emulates your life
When at each turn look upward, perceive beauty in stained light

The convoluted labyrinth fills the centre of the knave
Once a point for pilgrims for the solace that it gave
Their tortuous ageless journey represented in the stone
Worn smooth coiled meanderings allude you're not alone

It represents your journey, cool path beneath your feet
And just like life, at every turn, there are others that you meet
Each direction new facade, stained glass exquisite and serene
And again like life hints of what your future and past may mean

Along its path, time to reflect, of times and those departed
Along with future expectations and a life as yet uncharted
Your walk may take only minutes or perhaps an hour or more
But affects you for eternity, an experience you can't ignore

At labyrinth's centre a final step, one I have yet to take
As my journey is not yet over, Chartres merely a break
I am certainly not religious, yet it was so profound for me
Therefore, I suggest to all that you visit yourselves and see

Chartres Cathedral, also known as Cathedral of Our Lady of Chartres, is a medieval Catholic cathedral located in Chartres, France, approximately 80 kilometres southwest of Paris.

The labyrinth of Chartres (which is also one of the largest of its type in the World) is situated in the knave of the cathedral and is also known as la lieue (or league: which is a distance of about three miles).

Although the length of the labyrinth's path is only 290 meters, it is suggested some pilgrims would walk the labyrinth on their knees. This undertaking would take about an hour, or the time needed to walk a league. For many of the faithful, walking the labyrinth was a substitute pilgrimage to the Holy Land.

Its spiritual intensity is heightened by the fact that no direct light enters the building. All the light is filtered through stained glass, so that the whole experience of visiting the Chartres Cathedral is enhanced.

The labyrinth of Chartres Cathedral is open for walking on Fridays between Lent and All Saints Days (February-November).

The flex

"I like to play with children". It was meant in the literal sense.
The atmosphere was ramped up, taut, nail-biting, tense.
His be-suited brief beside him looked uncomfortable in his role.
Words spoken by his client, made him work to keep control.

The interview room was basic some would say austere,
But that all fell by the wayside as words spoken with a sneer.
The black topped wooden table and recorder there to see.
Discarded plastic tape wraps, a red blinking LED.

"The children liked it really, they'd do anything for treats.
I didn't do them any harm, the kids did it for the sweets.
I took them to the store room, at the rear of the main shop.
They were quiet, non-objected, no one asked for me to stop".

Kept my hands upon the table, must keep myself in check.
The cable to the telephone would fit nicely round his neck.
I grip my pen so tightly my knuckles turning white.
My tone still falsely calm, quiet and polite.

That cable could be my failure, curled against the wall.
It would take so little effort for me to lose it all.
The thought is tempting perhaps few would object.
But he'd be the winner, my career would be wrecked.

Our eyes across the table, he looked but could not see.
He'd done nought that he thought wrong as he stared across at me.
That frightening fact unsettling, but at least it meant he'd talk.
Evidence emerging slowly, but free he would not walk.

He did of course, freed on bail before the case was heard,
A community with different agendas now galvanised and stirred.
His shop was daubed and damaged, vigilantes did their stuff.
Mostly vandals who don't give a shit, others who'd heard enough.

Two years in prison, but we know that that means one.
A lifetime for the kids, childhood completely gone.
Virtually all in isolation, rule 43 it's called,
Only because the other lags find themselves appalled.

I've won a little battle, but I haven't won a war.
As I know for in my future, there will always be one more.
He'll start again in a few years' time, with rippling effects.
And then when I hear, I will once more think;
"I should have used that flex".

High roller

You've heard it before and it cannot be denied
Life's an extended roller coaster ride
Little command of direction, swirls, twists and turns
And just like that first drop, there are huge concerns

There are moments of excitement, pure exhilaration
Competing with darkness, fear, consternation
Times when the run seems out of control
When the turn of events should be viewed as a whole

Convoluted conveyor with more than one trough
But at least at the end you are not left to drop off
It's a ride best enjoyed, in the arms of a friend
Because just as with age, it slows down at the end

When that final straight looms have no regrets
Remember those high points and shared sunsets
It's a ride that must finish, as all journeys do
Which is why I reiterate, it's better ridden as two

Noisy bodies

A snore is a noise we unwillingly make,
which confirms that we are asleep.
A resonance that often keeps others awake,
whilst announcing our slumber is deep.

A fart is a noise, ill-mannered and smut,
a sound used in comedy farce.
It alleviates pressure from inside our gut,
it's a shame that the valve is our arse.

A cough is a noise, a respiratory fight,
which we also can use to disturb.
If deliberately done, and the timing is right,
It's a feat that leaves others perturbed.

A burp is a noise that melodiously says,
we have eaten and savoured our food.
In places, considered a way to show praise,
in others, incredibly rude.

A sneeze is a noise, causing nostrils to flare,
at one time meant plague or TB.
In modern times highlights our allergy scares,
caused by pollen, peanuts or Brie.

A creak is a noise, alluding old age,
and indicates joints become weak.
In our body, arthritis begins to rampage,
yet our youth we continually seek.

A sigh is a noise, unassuming and small,
but confirms we're alive and have breath.
But all of these noises mean nothing at all,
to someone entirely deaf.

Anita

Anita's amateur dramatics would make her parents proud
A teenager with social skills stood her well above the crowd.
Rehearsal finished, she'd catch her bus, West Brom homeward bound
Pop in the shops before the ride, her routine safe and sound.

Anita walked across the road no vehicle did she see
Though one was there, 'twas long way off, you'd certainly agree.
Car appeared 'long Hollyhedge Road, speed limit set at thirty.
Velocity was not that slow, he was travelling far too quickly.

At night, perspective should be good, lights larger it would seem
Although perhaps a little blurred even if on main beam.
But well away, as she started to cross, no need to hurry up.
Yet within only seconds her body would be struck.

First witnesses they heard the bang and turned more in despair
Yet did not see Anita, for she was in the air.
The car struck her hard at sixty four, chance she never stood
But he never even thought to halt as normal people would.

He stopped nearly a mile away, impact sensor forced that choice.
While running saw a mate of his, now haunted by this voice.
"I think I have just killed someone" slurred speech was heard to utter.
In fact almost every human bone lay broken in the gutter.

Limbs ripped off, the rag doll lay, reconstruction I would do
Although the worst is not the blood, it's telling parents too.
He bragged he'd get away with it, whilst in the pub once more.
Cared not about the family left, downed his pints just like before.

He would even plead not guilty, said drank after to calm his nerves.
Dragged her family, and many others, through ordeal that none deserves.
Convicted yes, but what a joke, remorse not once displayed.
Out in less than two years, her family felt betrayed.

They let him out for Christmas, lest his family be upset,
Whilst Anita's family mourned some more, he showed no regret.
She's not the first, and not the last, of re-cons that I've done.
But even when they get sent down, I never feel I've won.

Infant to child and beyond

"I'm so fed up". "I wish I was dead".
Phrases I hear, words that I dread.
Depressed, lethargic.
But the truth has been said.

Wants to go out, once out to go home.
Spurning company, ultimately alone.
Insular, indifferent.
Contented to moan.

Always kind and courteous, particularly caring,
But attitude now is increasing wearing.
Hostile, thoughtless.
Mood swings from ageing.

Bizarre conversations, repetitious or wild,
Recurrent like nightmares, thoughts misfiled.
Downhearted, dejected.
Infant to adult, adult to child.

Can it get better or be only agony?
Dementia's onset the unstoppable malady.
Illogical, amnesic.
A devastating tragedy.

The concluding episode, ensuing shell from person.
Cancer's clandestine grip begins to tighten.
Creeping, unstoppable.
The final curtain.

The Battle of La Moucheron

With dusk arrives hostilities,
battle lines are drawn.
Struggles rage throughout the night,
continuing 'til dawn.

Under cover of the darkness
the fight is played like chess,
Tarantella-like manoeuvrings,
no slumber and no rest.

We make our preparations
not trenches, bunkers, bombs,
but pills and creams and aerosols,
we know the foe will come.

We smear our skins with lotions,
even utilise a mesh.
Still the enemy's persistent
to achieve its pound of flesh.

They seek out heat like radar,
infrared to view its prey.
Despite our best defences
we get bitten come what may.

Morning reveals the glory
of the plot that they did hatch,
and we all end up scratching
at that very itchy patch.

The mosquito is the victor
and it's not an aeroplane.
It's a pesky little midge fly,
who wins the fight, again!

The beach

The beach is such a wondrous place.
It sings, it speaks
you walk, it squeaks

Buckets and spades, when once a child.
Castles to build
Fantasies fulfilled

Slowly we walk, unwind, relax.
Sun on our skin
A smile within

The beach will remain, beyond our being.
I have no regrets
Watching sunsets

Ham and Pasta

Penne pasta with ham, cooked in port,
with Philly and an extra swirl of cream.
A gentle squeeze of the knee
and a hand resting comfortably on the thigh,
casual caresses meaning more than they seem.

Watching the pink and persimmon sunset
sink beyond the horizon, from smooth golden sand.
Another moment of outstanding beauty
meaningless, unless it is shared,
together hand in hand.

The gentle nuzzle of a nose in an ear,
times of conversation with your best friend.
Moments of companionable silence
when words need not be spoken,
mere presence is enough to transcend.

For one the sound of keys in the door
still makes the heart skip and flutter.
For the other, childlike excitement on the journey home
becomes a challenge to restrain,
knowing as the years go by, our love grows stronger.

Personal moments of exhilaration and emotion,
excitement setting the pulse rate faster.
These points in time will always outweigh by far,
the unimaginable inevitability;
there will be no more ham with pasta.

No instructions supplied

Consuming and expensive, but your life is richer.
They devour you but you still want to give more.
You strive to do what is right,
you go out on a limb and you wonder,
what did we ever do before?

You do all you can but there are no rules,
no manual to study, to get it right first time.
With no second chance you gamble,
play the percentage odds, and do what you think is best.
It's not a fairy tale and there's no 12 o'clock chime.

There is no quantifiable measure of your success,
you know nothing materialistic can be a guide.
All you want is for them to interact, show compassion and care.
They do and that is how you acknowledge who they are.
It is not what they do; it's what they are inside.

Tell them, "Do it now, you may not be able when ties are made"
but you fear for their future and what it will hold.
Hope they account for what is yet to come
and when they plan, hope ultimately
they do what they think is right, not what they are told.

Meals, no matter what the time or weather,
the flicker of candles make it something special.
Two, three or four dining, it makes no difference.
Never miss out on the opportunity, to be as one,
be friends, sit and eat and converse around the table.

You watch your children, wishing and trying your best.
What they have become makes you proud.
They may seem anonymous in the grand scheme.
But, knowing who they really are inwardly
makes them stand out from the crowd.

The motor car

For some it inspires a poem,
the chancellor exploits it for tax.
For others it's used as a mode to win,
for a few, a route to relax.

The car is such an enigma,
it takes as well as gives,
for something so mechanical,
you'd think it almost lives.

Its emissions try to choke us,
it vomits death and dirt,
it costs us all a fortune,
but it's our lives it really hurts.

One million pounds per fatal,
they say that is the cost,
but really it is family life
that suffers the greatest loss.

There's no monetary cost to tragedy,
it's the supreme price that we pay.
Wasted lives, young and old,
taken every single day.

Metal, perversely, caresses our bodies,
ribs kiss and then puncture our lungs.
The arteries tear, the lungs they burst,
blood spews across our tongues.

Healthy bones snap, as they hit the dash,
the car stops; our organs keep moving.
The NHS tries to use what is left,
but the heart is so subject to bruising.

Destruction of family, that is the real price,
not the metal, the plastic or transport.
It's the funerals and grief, the tears and the strife,
not the cost at the pump on the forecourt.

We try to be eco, to save the world,
fuels we strive to improve,
but our planet still suffers, as well as our lives,
in the end, all of us lose.

For some it inspires a poem,
others it may take their breath.
The car drives us to our independence,
but ultimately, propels us to death.

The 'A' pillar

The arm burst violently through the windscreen
Its trajectory wildly intractable and unforeseen
The flaccid black and leather clad limb
Alluding of a future, predisposed and grim

Motorcycle continued like a rider-less plough
Destruction sought in its final bow
Rider in pain, afraid, feeling colder
Looks in anguish at his limbless shoulder

'A' pillar of the van an unsought edged blade
Cutting through bone, tendons and skin frayed
Laminate failing, absorbing like a trap
Retarding the limb 'til it fell on his lap

Fragment and splinters of glass filled the air
Adding to discomfort, shock and despair
Blood splattered road revealing its own story
Later explained to a spellbound jury

Life changing injuries, life changing vision
Life changing outlook follows the collision
A moment of madness preceded by drink
Impacts like ripples, to make us all think

Concluded at court finalised in law
Insurance paid out discussed no more
Yet well beyond now memories will remain
Of the sights and the sounds, the emotions and pain

Fulfilled

The pulse of the waves
Feathered accompaniment in trees
Soothing rolling music
reassuring to me.

Breast cupped in hand
Spooning gently in bed
The utterance of peace
Requiring nought said.

Clear sky azure blue
The sweet smell of pine
Ultimate relaxation
Fulfilment mine.

As I lie and embrace
Try and understand why
All I want is to smile
Yet the same time, cry

Morphology

(Rote buy Keith Terry)

Poetry's easy when ewe no watt too rite.
Words then floe easy lea, a beauty full site.
English, the language we yews on the page,
in a whey understood, know matter yore age.

Of coarse it's am big you us, sew wee say what we mean,
and seems aren't quite litter rally just watt they seam.
Portmanteau of sum words is easy two sea,
but port man tow in others, owe wear can it bee?

Words can be small, butt there meaning is their,
other words sew big, they jump out and stair.
Sum words are long, and very morpheme,
and why isn't phonics spelt how it's scene?

Sesquipedalian has syllables to spare,
it's reel lea a hum bull word but with pretentious flare.
It's sub stance that matters not just the sound,
sew lets keep words simple, try knot two confound.

It is a strange language, that wee don't no well.
It twists and it terns, but wear we can't tell.
Their is one thing with English that aye must con seed
as long as it's red write it's easy two reed.

Montalivet

Monta is excitement, yet tranquil in its calm.
An isle of peace and solitude, when together arm in arm.
There are no airs or graces, you must take as you will find,
In a place not of appearances, but of truth and of the mind.

English rarely spoken; the language of life reigns supreme,
Giving deeper understanding of what life really means.
Yet time here flies by quickly, as we work, relax and love,
With colours clear and vivid, enhanced by blue above.

The rat race is suspended; hours can last for days,
To relax an understatement, in many different ways.
A way of life so natural, it's hard to wonder why,
Everyone who's pressured doesn't live this way, or try.

The air is fresh, pine-scented, the atmosphere rich, yet clear.
Friendships made through short exchange, go on to last for years.
A cacophony of silence, of birds, of breeze, of sea.
A place to spend a lifetime, if you are here with me.

Defining moments

In memory of Chris 'Woody' Bradshaw.
Killed racing at the Isle of Man
September 1, 2010

"Life can be so cruel",
"You only have one life, live it".
Expressions such as these are easy to say,
but life is surely tenuous
it can be quickly snatched away.

One moment all is well,
the next, finality bites.
Exhilaration can be another's despair.
Whilst nothing should be begrudged,
grief does not play fair.

For one, it's the end,
for another, new challenge.
The moment in time for each so defining.
It may be a new dawn,
but presently, there is no sun shining.

Whilst some can escape,
others come together to support.
One step too far, is it luck or just fate?
We all know life can be so cruel,
We just find out too late.

How lucky I am!

How lucky am I
at this moment in time?
Whilst reflecting my fortunes
others struggle to survive.

How lucky am I
whilst others are dying?
I relax by the sea,
in dappled shade, lying?

How lucky am I
whilst at home people grieve?
I escape from it all
and reality I leave?

How lucky am I
as life so swiftly alters?
Make the most of it now
lest your body, it falters.

How lucky am I?
I hope that I know.
Whilst here I'm cocooned,
my friends they still go.

How lucky I am
my life's riches have grown,
through the ones I share life with,
and friends lucky to have known.

Perfection

As I sit here in dappled shade,
sunlight filters through rambutan trees.
Coucher du soleil is but an hour away.
Shadows long, light intense,
vivid colours fight for prominence.

Not a human sound can be heard.
The cacophony of stillness is interwoven
with incessant rushing waves,
gently caressing golden sands nearby.
Wisps of abstract white punctuate almost endless azure sky.

Swallows dance upon the faintest of breezes.
Finches and other passerines converse amongst themselves,
though we are privileged to eavesdrop.
Warning, calling, but above all, singing.
Rejoicing in late May's, early summer evenings.

I close my eyes; perfection.

The Red Wheelbarrow

William Carlos Williams
1883 – 1963

so much depends
upon

a red wheel
barrow

glazed with rain
water

beside the white
chickens

The Red Wheelbarrow

Inspired by "The Red Wheelbarrow"
written by William Carlos Williams
1883 – 1963.

The rain-glazed wheelbarrow
was not actually red.
It was dry and mud coated,
more light brown instead.
As for the chickens,
not one could be seen.
In fact, the whole farmyard
had lost so much of its sheen.

The rain that once glazed it,
on which all life depends,
causes decomposition,
even death in the end.
Oxide, corrosion,
continued abuse.
From initial dependence,
to no further use.

Holed, leaking and wobbly,
neglected and spurned.
Now used as a shelter,
ignored and upturned.
So no more white chickens,
no barrow of red.
But Williams' poem?
It's stuck in my head.

Fifty quid

Redundancy discussed today, I came home feeling crap.
Do I apply or do I wait? It's like being in a trap.
I watch the news at six o'clock, see starving people fall,
Now I feel bad, for feeling crap, my troubles are so small.

"You have some post, it came today, I'll bring it in," says she.
No bills, no flyers, no junk mail, just one addressed to me.
I slit the top, I now feel worse, I know what it contains.
Médecins Sans Frontières, a charity without chains.

Donation due, my cheque they need, the one I send each year.
It's not a lot, just fifty quid, my feelings now quite clear.
What's fifty here, or fifty there? At least I have the choice,
Unlike the displaced masses who don't even have a voice.

Emotions change, realisation sad, my own plight is not hard.
My kids don't die through lack of food. I buy that on a card.
I'll send it off, what's fifty pounds? It may save someone's life.
I really am a lucky man, my family, my health, my wife.

Nude sunbathing.

I lie in the sunshine, my bits hanging down,
Heat searing my nose, like an overweight clown.
I should really be bronzing, protected by cream.
For my health and my comfort, factor twenty sunscreen.

But it's late afternoon, sun's starting to sink,
I'm feeling all dreamy, skin turning pink.
Resigned to a red nose, I'm really, "So what!"
My concern really should be, what else will get hot?

There's obvious etiquette for Ambre-Solaire,
Pertaining application to a place; you know where.
Forgive me I beg you, I try not to be crude,
But applying my sunscreen, to some, may seem rude.

It's not that I want to, but necessity calls.
My bits just get warmer, especially my balls.
So I've made a decision, the moment has come.
There's nothing else for it; get out of the sun!

The beach is!

The beach at Monta is;
Fine golden grains, relaxes, sustains.
Feeds the soul, makes one whole.
Air on the skin, enhances within.
It is just...
It just is.

Peace

Sunlight filters through intense emerald foliage.
These beams from Heaven caress my skin.
Fearful of my true motives for being here
A pearl of saltiness falls to my page
There is nothing here I need
Yet all I need is here.
Hand in hand.
Tranquillity.
Peace.

Nothing

There are times when life is wonderful
When mere presence is enough.
There are times when nothing need be said,
. . . .

How is life measured?

Life is not measured by the breaths we take,
Though lengthened or shortened by decisions we make.
It's not measured in minutes, hours or by days,
Not even in years or countless other ways.

It's not measured in money or material wealth,
Though the years may pass easier if enjoyed in good health.
It's not measured in property, possessions or stocks,
By collections of jewellery, art or gold blocks.

It's not measured by Cartier, or fast flashy cars,
And surely not by holidays taken afar.
Travel may enlighten and broaden our minds,
But it's still not a measure of our life and our times.

No, our life is not measured by those breaths that we take,
Though it may be enhanced by the friends that we make.
There is only one method, ne'er what others say,
It's measured by the moments that take our breath away.

What is life?

Without its downs, life has no ups,
a voyage across a sea.
There are many swells and numerous lows
that's the harsh reality.

So what is life, this time we're here,
these facets of which we speak?
The ingredients of a meal so rich,
the main course that we seek?

Living, a rainfall of discovery
that's pointless unless shared.
A voyage etched upon the heart
from a journey unprepared.

Happiness, shared sunsets,
witnessed hand in hand.
Whether over urban landscapes
or beyond soft golden sands.

Grief, of trying to save a life
and in the process failing.
There's no instructions how to live,
it cannot be plain sailing.

Contentment, if we find it,
when nothing need be said.
A nod, a smile, a knowing look,
a brief caress instead.

Love, childlike excitement,
when travelling home each day.
A quickened pulse, a silly grin,
which words just can't convey.

Sadness stems from unwanted fate,
inevitable but true.
We leave our love as only one,
having entered there as two.

Lives, like stories, all must end.
When and how, who knows?
The details are there, but unlike text,
the reader never knows.

The blackbird and the pussycat

The blackbird eyes the rambutan
With berries lavish red.
The feline eyes the chirping bird,
Plans forming in her head.

A game of cat and mouse ensues
Though no rodent in this play.
A chaffinch looks on from afar;
He'll survive another day.

The ripened fruit disturbed by beak
Falls gently to the ground.
The blackbird descends, to find its meal.
The cat makes not a sound.

The blackbird pecks, luscious fruit exposed,
It satiates its needs.
The cat stalks slowly, stealth in mind,
Whilst the blackbird picks out seeds.

But a call rings out, a chirrup loud,
A warning from up high.
Alarm is raised, and none too soon,
Cat spotted from the sky.

The fruit abandoned swiftly.
Wits pitched another time.
These antics a mere instalment.
The entertainment, mine.

Solace

I lie in bed and listen,
Through windows hear the sea,
Cloudless sky, blue as can be,
And I smile inwardly.

Beyond the shutters, trees of Pine,
Bright sunshine beckons me,
Soul laid bare for all to see,
Drawn here so inexorably.

In the future, portal closes,
A fact of life invariably,
until that moment, heavenly
When gone, no matter, I am free.

The biggest insect in the world; ever!

I saw an insect this afternoon,
The biggest I've ever seen.
Antennae just like tentacles
of something more marine.

There may be bigger kept in zoos
On my terrace, it's something new.
It wasn't right to swat it dead
To this giant, what to do?

I know, thought I, I'll take a pic,
Then none can doubt my claim.
I crept off, got my camera.
For evidence I could frame.

Macro setting, that will do,
So I can get close up.
Result? A photo that was blurred.
I wasn't close enough.

A few more shots, I clicked away.
Evidence without fail.
I put a ruler by its side.
Perspective now, and scale.

It scurried fast on sensing me,
Ran at me 'cross the floor.
I jumped and crushed it underfoot.
The insect was no more.

An accident, it was not meant.
It ran beneath my feet.
I panicked for a second time.
On my camera pressed delete.

Yet this tale of size you must believe,
a behemoth, wings unfurled.
An insect rare in length and girth,
The biggest in the world!

How quiet?

The hush of a warm breeze, gentle creak of a bough.
Tiny crack of fir cone as it opens somehow.
Sweet call of a bird high up in a tree.
A scurrying gecko frightened of me.

A chirruped reply in the distance I hear.
All the sounds of silence, so still and so clear.
A butterfly dances, its ballet unheard,
As it fleets through the air, to the songs of the birds.

The schhh of the sea, caressing the beach.
Abstract white patterns float high out of reach.
So still is the day it's not hard to believe,
I hear pencil scratching paper, and can hear myself breathe.

Varicelle

This holiday was a different one, we looked forward to a rest.
We didn't know what was to come, to relax would be a test.
It started on the Saturday, with a day spent on the beach.
Come Sunday some small spots appeared, awkward ones to reach.

Was it sandflies from the dunes perhaps, the cause of her being bitten?
Strange 'cause I'd had, not one bite, with her skin they were smitten.
They itched through Sunday then got worse, oh dear, could it be fleas?
They covered back and legs and tum, I felt sorry for Louise.

I'd fumigate the bedroom, disinfect and clean up lots.
But the more I cleaned the more they spread. Louise was covered in spots.
It turned out to be chicken pox, for adults it is shingles.
Louise, she could not socialise, was not allowed to mingle.

The sun was such a godsend, Calamine a saving grace.
But as soon as visitors came close, covering spots was such a race.
Most neighbours kept their distance, but Pierre, aperitif?
We declined; at first bewilderment, realisation, then relief.

I tried not take the mickey, having shingles can be tough.
But just one little poem I'm sure will be enough.
For rest we came to Monta, now Louise she would get lots.
Whilst I went out and rode my bike, she stayed and hid her spots.

So I'm sorry if you're spotty, I know it's not much fun,
And while you're covered from head to toe, I'm afraid I don't have one.
But at least look on the bright side, it could be worse you see.
The person having all those spots, it could have been poor me.

Dave the clever bloke

I struggled with the concept of why wind should exist.
I thought I knew the theory, but the practice was a mist.
It's all to do with highs and lows, of pressure and of heat.
Of where there's one, the others not and sometimes where they meet.

My mate Dave, the clever bloke, did eloquently explain.
The whys and wherefores were complex, so went through it all again.
If pressure's low, it leaves a space, void filled with other air.
Of course I realised, but asked, "This other air's from where?"

The filling air's from somewhere high, he went on to expound.
That's pressure high, not altitude, it could be near the ground.
Ah! I see. I saw the light, understand now what you mean.
The wind's the movement of the air, just felt but can't be seen.

So where the high has come from, I presume the pressure drops.
Some other air replaces that, the cycle never stops.
"You've got it", said my learned friend, his face now looked less fraught.
A bloke so well informed is Dave, but then I had a thought.

Why can't the air just stabilise? I must have thought out loud.
For Dave gave me a pensive look, smiled, before he frowned.
Our rational, once poles apart, a connecting thread he fits.
Whilst top and bottom heat up less, sun warms the middle bits.

"The tropics", says Dave, "Get hotter. The poles they stay quite cold.
Air moves and tries to compensate". I reason what I'm told.
So there always will be movement and wind forever be.
And now I understand it all, 'cause Dave explained to me.

First aid for my soul

My past is catching up with me.
Contorted twisted bodies, bereft of their life
Cadavers on tables sliced up with a knife
Smears on a road surface, fractured white bones
Messages of death to distraught Mrs. Jones.

I know a place where I can hide.
The problem with hiding is time able to think
Of the moments in life that can turn you to drink
Hours cathartic help get over distress
Allow you to cope having relived the mess.

Rose-tinted spectacles perhaps required.
Clouds are few and far between, the sun is always warm
Winter months of forced neglect produce a perfect lawn
The sea is calm inviting, reached 'cross golden, pristine sand
My vestige of reality is walking hand in hand.

Imagination or pragmatism.
An isle where we can hide away, escape from fear and crime
Live quiet and elemental, where light dictates time
It frightens me, if truth be known, medicate to help me cope
Escape cannot be permanent but at least I now have hope.

First aid for the soul.
Such panaceas do exist of that I am now sure
They are the best of bandages, if not perhaps the cure
A way of life lived long or short, a pace slow and sublime
A place that I can share with love,
A place I can call mine.

Escape to reality

A place so calm and natural, no superficial grime.
A place so true and basic where light dictates the time.
A place to live in harmony, restfulness and peace.
A place that makes you cry with joy, does such a place exist?

A place where birds keep singing in sunshine and in rain.
A place where you can stay relaxed, devoid of hurt and pain.
A place where life is started, a place to wonder, why?
A place to contemplate and reflect, perhaps a place to die.

A place so full of wonderment, yet simple in extremes.
A place where you can sit and think, of what life really means.
A place of changed priorities, relevance less clear.
A place where souls can be unlocked, friendships become dear.

A place so easy to be found, yet so hard to define.
A place so true it must be false and only of the mind.
Yes this place does exist for me, it resolves and reassures,
I've found my place, my sanity; you should strive to find yours.

Sun v clouds

White wisps collude with voluminous abstract patterns of grey,
Eager to obscure perceived sapphire above.
Combining in their conflict, grey deepens from ash to charcoal.
Even the sun fails in its battle of luminosity,
Retreating without movement, to fight another day.
Sun gives way for clouds to rain.

Regrouped for battle, the sun responds.
Joints and beams creak in combined defiance,
In answer to the sun's unceasing efforts.
The sun evokes and invigorates our world with its persistence.
Fiery strength powering its way through monochrome ramparts.
Cloud gives way for sun to reign.

Rose-tinted spectacles?

The nose is pressed against the windows of the soul.
Searching inward and discovering secrets and desires,
To complete and make perfect, even the unprocurable.
A wish to fulfil, assist or even cajole.

We sit together, absorbed in each other's tasks.
In a place so natural, but in reality so fake.
We hide away in plain sight, heads buried in our openness,
Blissfully unaware, so easy to relax.

We put off the inevitable, savour the diversion.
View through metaphorical rose-tinted spectacles,
Satiate our desires, put dark thoughts aside.
Make the most of short-lived perfection.

We hope we have long, lazy, love filled days ahead.
Yet perfection is always: just around the corner.
As we look into our souls, those corners ebb closer.
While we wait and grow older, little needs to be said.

Listening to nothing

Have you ever noticed how loud silence can be?
Echoes of silence everywhere seem so subtle to me.
Wind whispering through branches, faint creek of a bough,
Hearing yourself breathe, softly thunderous somehow.

The crisp sharp split of pine cones, a swift static sound.
Seeds of life spiral downward, caressing the ground.
Flight ending softly, a sojourn swiftly spun.
Joining late summers carpet, brittle from sun.

Small squirrels search skittish through this dry vegetation.
Scratching so seraphic, lifeblood their elation.
Merest hint of a hoot disappear in a thrice.
Then returning to snuffle, like elegant mice.

Throughout all this clamour of minuscule sound,
A rumble surging constant, portending profound.
Alluding to mechanical, a subdued rhythmic train?
Moon's heartbeat needs no clouds, rolls again and again.

Crickets sing rhythmically, percussive, not oral.
Their pitched variations, pulsatingly choral.
A movement heard, chirruping ceases.
Stillness returns, conversations repeated.

Listening to nothing needs no special ability.
To be comforted by calm, love peace and tranquillity.
Listen to nature's magnificent voice.
Listen with deference, make silence a choice.

My owl

I listened to an owl last night as I lay in bed, awake,
Amazed by piercing clarity of the eerie cries they make.
The sound of running water from a toiling stream nearby,
Subtle, gentle, whispers of trees, backdropped by sky.

Preoccupied by movement of dark and brooding clouds,
As moonlight silvered abstract shapes form ghostly floating shrouds.

Cutting through, the owl persists, perchance a mate to find,
I eavesdrop so intently, thoughts coursing through my mind .
Then all at once the screeching ceased, silhouette caught my eye.
Owl's background, now a steely black, moon luminous and high.

Framed by stars, it casts its glow, a sinister spectral light.
Clouds now gone, air is sharp, silent, chromatic, bright.

The clamour that was silence played out inside my head,
As I waited there expectantly, breathing shallow in my bed.
My mind alert, on tenterhooks, through hours long and late,
Was calmed once more on hearing, owl calling for a mate.

Sound may have been more distant but it gave my soul a lift.
Relaxed and feeling comforted, to sleep I could now drift.

It was no accident!

Road accidents, I would dare to imply,
are as rare as rocking horse shit.
Accidents no, there's invariably fault,
collision, the word I submit.

Drivers the problem, what is it they cause?
They thoughtlessly bring forth death.
Roads play no part, yet are blamed to the enth,
you cannot catch your breath.

What actually happens, in these collisions?
How fractured do lives become?
The impact, is not all metallic in force,
it's grief and anguish to which we succumb.

Airbags explode; endeavour to protect,
yet ruptured chests still buckle the wheel.
Adrenaline surges, anaesthesia fails,
pain induced by twisted steel.

Metal, perversely, caresses our bodies;
ribs kiss, then puncture our lungs.
The arteries tear, our lungs they burst,
blood spews across our tongues.

Healthy bones snap, as they hit the dash.
The car stops, but our organs keep moving.
Whilst limbs are violently ripped apart,
internally, constrictive crushing.

Faces try travel, 'twixt the roof and screen,
route hindered by mirrors and visors.
Laminate screens seeks to contain,
shredding skin like twin-bladed razors.

Smears on the road, crimson clues to the cause,
though the reason, invariably speed.
Perhaps lack of concentration,
or inconsiderate self-centred greed.

Critical speed, pedestrian throw,
skid tests to help us explore;
coefficient of friction, expressed in mu,
to find speeds and understand more.

Mutilation merely precursor,
to agony returning again.
Ripples on ponds radiate hurt,
mental anguish following pain.

One million pounds, the measure of fatals,
the attributed monetary cost.
In reality, many family lives suffer
incalculable, undeserved loss.

The truth, in fact, is plain for us to see,
the price: unacceptably high.
Yet we still see those fools, every day.
All we can do is ask, "Why?"

Hope in the sky

Life is like the sky;
azure blue,
hope at its zenith.
Clouds may temporarily blur and obscure hope.
Hidden behind white or grey
wispy or voluminous,
life's myriad of pathways
mere clouds floating by.
You may travel through dark storm clouds
at times in your life,
however,
when they have blown away,
as all clouds surely do,
hope returns,
the strongest of blue.
No matter what the weather throws at us
blue is always there.
In life blue is constant.
You can never live life without hope.

Waking

Looking through the window of my escape
I see treetops waving to me almost imperceptibly.
Pine cones now appear
like gilt chromatic gems caressing emerald fronds
as dawn caresses the branches of another new day.

The pernicious early morning feathered chorus
ravishes my ears.
High-pitched chatter and song interspersed with doves cooing like
lovers.
These crusades of passion are echoed by a backdrop
of the ocean's continual caressing of sand.
Lying prostrate I struggle to hear my own breathing
against nature's clamour.

Sunlight slowly floods into my room,
Heat pours through open shutters
Wisps of white wend their way across cerulean blue
Before disappearing like disembodied spirits
Simmering warmth despatches their feeble efforts
to be a part of this fresh start.
My escape is complete; or is it?

Open eyes

Over my life there's been volumes to see
Frequently, perhaps, too much for me.
Watching someone burning, trapped and then die,
Blurring eyes, held back, powerless to try.

Murdered bodies of children, left to be found,
A shocking indictment, effects so profound.
Desperation, panic, etched on one too many faces,
Seen on so many people, so many places.

Jumpers from high-rise, 13th floor to the ground,
Haunting dull thud, a deafening wet sound.
Waxen faced eyes, lifeless blank stare,
Searching for hope when they felt none was there.

Twisted metal and limbs should not be entwined,
Yet innumerable images reside in my mind.
Visions replayed of open none seeing eyes,
The signature sign of a grotesque demise.

It is said, "Without downs there cannot be ups",
Suggesting smooth sojourns which disorder interrupts.
Those spiralling lows evoke zenith high spheres,
Lifting life out of mundane, imparting salt-laced tears.

Keith Terry

Would I trade these deep lows? You would think I'd say "Yes",
But I'd lose wide-eyed moments I'd not want to suppress.
The birth of a child, lives we can cherish,
Outweigh those moments of when others did perish.

The finding of love, being loved in return,
Eclipse the sheer horror of watching someone else burn.
The sunsets, the tenderness, the sweet smell of pine,
The sharing, the serenity, with eyes open are mine.

These moments of bliss, of passion so pure
Are more than a match for those troughs we endure.
Glimpses into madness need not be missed,
They enable you to close your eyes, experience true bliss.

Life meanders onward, paths I can't foresee,
Twisting and reshaping, eye-opening for me.
I've been helped through my life by friends living and known.
Seen through open eyes, I am not on my own.

Lost and found

Crimson walls and furniture
Painted by wrists
Deliberately
Desperately twice slit.

Eyes now closed to a world
On someone who perceived
They did not
And could not fit.

Blood-scented air permeates
A neglected room
Corroding Gillette discarded
Death discernible all around.

A dejected soul
Sitting, slumped
Lost in mind
Waiting to be found,

But not by me.

The challenge

I have a challenge
The challenge unfolds;
The challenge is me.

I sense my head may burst
Random
Repeated
Resized thoughts
Race uncontrolled;
The challenge is me.

Desperately tired
Sleep deprived
Grip tenuous
Ever-changing
Trying to be strong and in control
Struggling to control oneself;
The challenge is me.

Family honesty prevails
I am privileged
Assisted
Loved
Challenge shared
And yet;
The challenge is still me.

The voyage etched on my heart

Isn't it wonderful how we now live so much longer; No.
There is much to see
Much to do in such a short time
Yet not when we sail so interminably slow.

A ship is beginning to sink
But am I the captain in the brink?
We flounder but persevere as we have no choice
No instructions, no directions, no compass, no guiding voice.

We know we must, and will, get through this surging voyage
Though cannot discern the scale of time.
Such arbitrary estimations, protracted or diminutive
Are no friends of mine.

The storm builds, a swirling tempest
But I have no sand in which to bury my head.
Information comes at me as wind from all directions
But I am surrounded by water instead.

Life belts are invariably thrown from those closest
Answering an unbeknown, pernicious distress flare.
Guilt, duty and love conflict like icebergs
With much below the surface of which we should be aware.

Eventually you come to terms and recognise
The imperative need to believe in and think of your crew.
As without their assistance and support on-board
There cannot hope to be a rescue.

Pull together, short strokes, deliberate, measured
Our lifeboat slowly and gradually moves from harm's way.
Ensuring a future for first mate, crew and passengers
We sail, perchance against the tide, but onward and away.

We continue and row on regardless, is all wonderful?
Can I convince myself, can I be truthful?
I look forward to that future when all is serene.
If and when that arrives, what will it entail, what will it mean?

The enemy within

If you look into a mirror
you see the enemy within
view sequences and episodes
of where little doubts begin

The person inside your psyche
by which your whole life is defined
has a myriad of methods
to infiltrate your mind

Is it destiny or is it luck
how our outcome is decided?
Whilst our being meanders onward
lost, afraid, unguided

Do I know? Am I aware?
perhaps I'm beyond caring
I despair of my foe within
Becoming all-consuming and ensnaring

I know nothing

I know I will grow old
I know that I will fall
I know I may feel weak at times
Frightened, tired and small

I know I'll probably break some bones
Know at times I may be ill
I know that I'll forget some things
Know life may become less of a thrill

I know my life will be subject to change
But one thing scares me today
It's when I don't know I know nothing
When I don't know what to say

I don't want to reach that dementia state
I've seen the awful effect
Of someone who once caring and clever
Without awareness and intellect

When I reach the point of not knowing
I know I will not know
But the one thing I hope I can achieve
Is to know when I must let go

Rain, rain go away,
come again another day

Rain is the giver of life
Yet corrodes with the merest of touch.
It nourishes, cleans,
And is more than it seems.

Without, arid lands lie barren.
Stunted growth sending roots far below.
Plants wither then fall
must evolve to grow tall.

In excess, rain wields great power.
We watch in wonder, cower in awe.
Giver and taker
Sustainer and breaker.

Nature's greatest gift is clear,
Benignant onslaught, heralds decay.
It feeds as it kills.
Is a solver of ills.

So will it kill or keep alive,
When nature's wondrous gift arrives?

Keith Terry

Could I? No I couldn't

A squirrel, a rodent, a grey furry rat
Yet it's just so difficult to think like that
A four-legged gnawer, coarse-haired vermin
A mindset inextricably hard to determine

A long fluffy tail, a really cute face
It jumps 'cross branches with feline grace
It sits back on its haunches nibbling a nut
Precocious, attractive, clever, but

It digs holes in our back lawn, buries its stash
Watches us in the garden bold as brass
Uproots the flower bulbs, chews carrots we've planted
From under the netting it's craftily lifted

But we enjoy their games as they chase round and play
To the point where we'll watch their activities all day
It's free entertainment the positive we accept
We need not do anything but enjoy them, except

Did I say free? That's not quite true, see
'Cus the man at the market laughed and told me
"You've spent over a tenner on his food and there's more
What about the squirrel box you bought off me before?"

I'd not thought like that, of the upfront cost
But it does stop me worrying they'd get hungry or lost
I top it up regular, the same time each day
And as soon as I whistle, they come from their dray

So it is free amusement, if I ignore what I pay
And just make the most of watching them play
Just keep off the veg, keep your dramas delightful
Or I might have to dust off my Remington rifle

Could I? No I couldn't

Life's a long song

"Life's a long song", said Jethro Tull
And he was right all along.
Our lives are a myriad of pathways,
Capably conveyed in song.

Our childhood days are nursery rhymes
Uplifting, unworried carefree.
Our teenage years push boundaries at times,
When you know everything, and everything's free.

Those become the Slipknot years
'Parent Advisory', on CD cases.
Screamed lyrics assault our wired-up ears,
KoRn with a K and white faces.

We don't want a job, no need to learn
Life's a long song with the drink.
Our lives turn inward, no concerns,
In fact no need to think.

Then responsibility with years arrives
Moody Blues come with age.
Subtler rock reflects our lives,
Melody replaces rage.

The volume often reduces
That's not to say the past was wrong.
I can see clearly now produces;
Life's a long song.

We move on toward the adult years
Births and marriage and loss.
Laughter and tears for souvenirs
Responsibilities and jobs.

Dancing in the dark in pubs
Late nights and revelry,
Becomes coffee bars and knitting clubs
And our sport's now on TV.

Hospital visits more frequent
Stairway to heaven comes along,
As we live beyond help and treatment,
Remember that life's a long song.

Darkness on the horizon

Darkness builds on the horizon
Voluminous portentous clouds assemble together
Their abstract screen blocks the endeavours of the sun.
I look to a future beyond that skyline
When the sunshine finally breaks through
Erasing the crepuscular covers
Brightening our world once more.
A new dawn
A new day
A resumed life.

Living life by the book

Am I a cowardly ostrich?
Perchance an escapee?
Is it possible to run away with a buried head?
Is it just me?

I try to be strong, but,
Alternatives few.
I must face the music
Sing to you.

Sticking plaster, recharge?
Short solace at best.
I know my shortcomings, so
Just preparatory rest.

Unknown, the future
Fear it, I may.
Often I am afraid.
What can I say?

All will be resolved
The future fixed.
I am luckier than most,
Yet feelings still mixed.

Next chapter, no synopsis,
No rough draft from above.
I will finished the book
Supported by love.

Five plus three equals silence

Five plus three equals silence
Dementia has its hold
No memory now of numbers
Tragic even for one now old

Five plus three equals naught
Blank like crossword squares
Vacant, never to be filled
Glazed, distracted stares

Five plus three equals nothing
Which is what the future holds
Borrowed time ticks away
Final weeks unfold

Five plus three equals silence
Colouring books beyond scope
Unable to read another sentence
Memory, life, beyond hope.

Morality and Honour

Society, less responsibility, invites spiralling abyss,
then honour and self-discipline invariably go amiss.
Departments that take care of us, they fight an unseen war,
dark and secret agencies, whose power grows more and more.

SO13 or MI5, never a descriptive name,
just faceless numbers telling nought of how they play their game.
They enlist the help of people, inconspicuous or renown,
some work for corporate businesses, all proud to defend the crown.

When things go wrong, as they often do,
what happens to these pawns?
They're abandoned, undefended, left to ruin, prison, scorn.
Cast aside, thrown to the wolves, help hears not their cries.
Broken, if not missing, and their version then denied.

Police, they scratch the surface, risk their lives to save the day,
but it's a no-win situation, with evidence often grey.
Information received, credible source, procedures followed through,
but if the wheel falls off, they carry the can,
their informant goes missing too.

It's agencies that do the deeds, it's they that get results.
The methods they use, that's something else,
who takes them to account?
More open now, or it would seem, window-dressing for the news,
but even departmental heads keep out of tactics used.

The democratic government arrogantly wipes its hands,
denying any knowledge of its secret service plans.
If results are good, I think we know, the blind eye it is turned,
with transparent deceit, they tell us their truth,
of how our freedom's been preserved.

Great freedoms for these agencies are given without candour,
but freedom needs those qualities, morality and honour.
What happens when these attributes are abused to keep us free?
Accountability and truth must win, lest descend to anarchy.

Instructions for writing Poetry

Sesquipedalian poetry,
Do we need to be so grand?
If little less articulate
Perhaps more may understand.

Such complicated verses
Made up with portmanteau
Smash onomatopoeia
Where metaphors fear to go.

Similes, like Plasticine
Build up morphology
But this literary morpheme world's
Not all it seems to be.

Pretty ugly oxymorons,
Can spice up dreary verse.
Whilst little light alliteration,
May brighten up drab or terse.

No need to be prosaic
There's no format style or rules,
No preserve of academics,
No requirement of tools.

Needs only pen and paper
With that pen let your thoughts flow.
Lay ideas on that parchment,
Persevere, you never know.

So complex rhymes or simple words,
It really is your choice.
Whatever; once in published print,
It becomes your written voice.

Finally the poem that sums everything up....

Lucky man

I really am so lucky
To have health, my love, my wife.
My children and my happiness,
In other words, my life.

FOOTNOTE

Many of these poems were conceived and written, as you may realise, either at Montalivet in the southwest of France, or with this bolt hole at the forefront of my mind.

Others were perhaps written at Monta for no other reason than I just happened to be there, and it is such an inspiring and relaxing place. I make no apologies for this small book of poems having, perhaps, a more than slight Gallic bias.

Keith Terry

NOTES

NOTES

Made in the USA
Charleston, SC
09 January 2016